Flight of the
Trumpeters

written by Lisa Norby

illustrated by Susan Kathleen Hartung

Mc Graw Hill **Macmillan**
McGraw-Hill

New York   Farmington

Two hundred years ago the skies were filled with the wild calls of trumpeter swans. Every autumn, large flocks of trumpeters would migrate from their homes in the northern states to wintering grounds as far south as Texas and Florida.

Maryland's Chesapeake Bay was another of the trumpeters' favorite wintering grounds. Long ago visitors to the area wrote of seeing huge flocks of these majestic birds landing on the bay. Up to 100,000 birds wintered on the Chesapeake at one time, which must have been an amazing sight!

Flight of the Trumpeters

written by Lisa Norby

illustrated by Susan Kathleen Hartung

THIS BOOK IS THE PROPERTY OF:

STATE _____

PROVINCE _____

COUNTY_____

PARISH _____

SCHOOL DISTRICT _____

OTHER _____

Book No._____
Enter information
in spaces
to the left as
instructed

ISSUED TO	Year Used	CONDITION	
		ISSUED	RETURNED
....	....		
....	....		
....	....		
....	....		
....	....		
....	....		
....	....		
....	....		

PUPILS to whom this textbook is issued must not write on any page or mark any part of it in any way, consumable textbooks excepted.

1. Teachers should see that the pupil's name is clearly written in ink in the spaces above in every book issued.
2. The following terms should be used in recording the condition of the book: New; Good; Fair; Poor; Bad.

Macmillan/McGraw-Hill

A Division of The **McGraw-Hill** *Companies*

Copyright © Macmillan/McGraw-Hill of McGraw-Hill Education
a Division of The McGraw-Hill Companies, Inc.

Macmillan/McGraw-Hill
Two Penn Plaza
New York, New York 10121

Book Design and Production: Kirchoff/Wohlberg, Inc.

Printed in the United States of America

ISBN 0-02-185281-2/5,U.6

7 8 9 006 04 03 02

Trumpeter swans are different from the swans we see in parks, zoos, and even in storybooks. These familiar swans are called mute swans. They were brought to America from Europe over one hundred years ago.

Mute swans are famous for their graceful curved necks. Nothing makes a prettier picture than a mute swan gliding along on a pond. Yet like many birds brought in from other parts of the world, mute swans are not always good for our environment. They drive away ducks and destroy underwater plants.

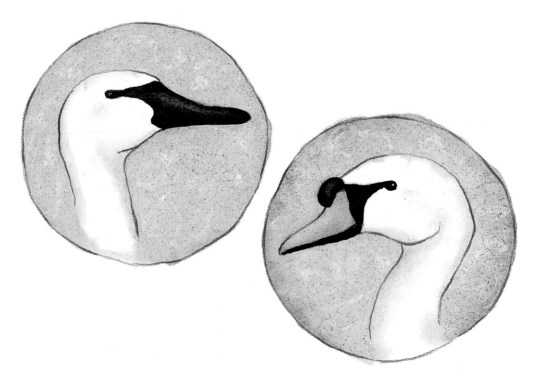

Trumpeter swans have straighter necks than mute swans, their bills are black, not orange, and they are larger than mute swans as well. An adult trumpeter weighs between twenty and thirty pounds. When it spreads its wings, the distance from wingtip to wingtip is over seven feet.

Young trumpeters choose a mate when they are about three or four years old and the pair of swans will stay together for life. Some swans live to be twenty years old or more.

Mute swans are quiet birds, but trumpeters are known for their deep call, which sounds like the blare of an old-fashioned horn or trumpet. The *ko-ho, ko-ho* sounds made by a flock of trumpeters flying overhead are unforgettable.

Hunters prized trumpeter swans—the swans' feathers were used for decorating ladies' hats and making powder puffs. So many trumpeters were shot that for years people thought they were extinct. In the early 1930s, however, sixty-six trumpeter swans were found living near hot springs in the Yellowstone National Park area. Later on, more trumpeters were found living in Alaska.

Scientists and bird lovers wanted to help the trumpeters. They started new flocks in several Midwestern states by bringing eggs and young birds from Alaska and Yellowstone.

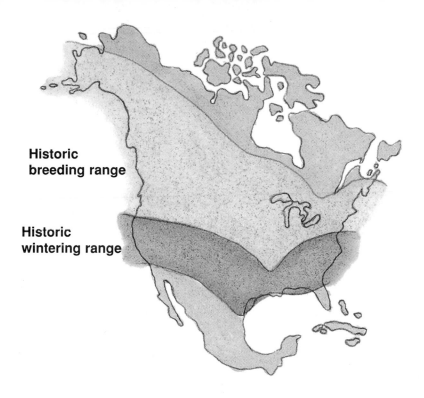

Historic breeding range

Historic wintering range

Birds in the new flocks face many dangers, however. Some trumpeter swans have perished after swallowing lead shotgun pellets. Today, we know that lead can poison birds, and hunters no longer use lead shots. Yet pellets from many years ago still lie buried in the mud bottoms of lakes and marshes. Trumpeters use their long necks to reach down into the mud, and some swallow enough lead to kill them.

Getting trumpeters to migrate to wildlife refuges where the marsh bottoms are free from lead would certainly help them. Unfortunately, this won't happen naturally. Like geese and other birds, swans aren't born knowing how to migrate. Young birds learn to navigate in the sky by following their parents. Today there are no adult birds left who know the old migration routes.

A few years ago, a Canadian named Bill
Lishman wondered if he could coax wild birds into
following a small airplane. Lishman owned an
ultralight aircraft that weighed just 250 pounds. It
looked like a hang glider with a seat and a small
motor attached.

Lishman also knew that some baby birds,
including geese and swans, assume that the first
thing they see after hatching is their mother. This
is known as *imprinting*. Lishman got some newly
hatched Canadian geese to imprint on him and his
aircraft!

In 1993 Lishman ushered a flock of wild geese
along a migration route of over 400 miles. The
flight started in Canada and ended in Airlie,
Virginia, and the story of this flight was made
into a movie called *Fly Away Home.*

Yet this 1993 migration was just the beginning of experiments with ultralight aircraft. Dr. William Sladen of the Environmental Studies Center in Airlie, Virginia, decided to see if the same idea would work with trumpeter swans.

Sladen and his team took seven eggs from trumpeter swans living at Airlie and kept them in an incubator.

A biologist named Gavin Shire was chosen to pilot the ultralight. Workers at Airlie did everything they could think of to make sure that their baby swans would imprint on Shire and his plane. Even before the swan eggs hatched, the workers began playing a tape recording of the sounds made by the airplane's motor!

The Airlie team also built a model of an ultralight. On the day the swans hatched the first thing they saw was Shire, standing with the model plane. The hatchlings accepted Shire as their mother!

Baby trumpeter swans, also known as *cygnets*, are covered with fluffy gray down. As soon as they are a day or two old, they are ready to leave their nest and explore their surroundings.

Shire walked around with the bottom section of the ultralight. Wherever he went, the cygnets would run after him.

Teaching the cygnets to fly with the ultralight was challenging. Young swans are clumsy fliers. They bumped into each other and flapped their wings wildly.

Shire's biggest challenge was teaching the swans to fly *behind* his ultralight, and not in front of it. Flying birds create air turbulence. The swans were so big and powerful that their flapping wings could have caused serious trouble for the pilot.

The stars of Shire's training flight were three female cygnets named Isabelle, Sidney, and Yo-Yo. They were chosen to take part in the first migration flight.

The test flight began in a Virginia cornfield early one December morning. Shire and his birds stopped once to rest. When nightfall came, they stopped again at a place called Magruder's Ferry.

The next morning they were off again. It was another beautiful, clear day and their route took them over Washington, D.C. When they reached the Chesapeake Bay, a Coast Guard vessel escorted them across the water. After a flight of 100 miles the birds reached their winter home on a Maryland farm.

Had the trumpeters learned the route well enough to make their way back home?

Yo-Yo was the first to leave her winter home. She had just landed for a rest when a woman saw her and decided that she must be in need of help. The woman meant well, but she put Yo-Yo in her yard where the young swan got into a fight with her pet dog. Isabelle and Sidney both followed the migration route but wandered off course.

All three trumpeters were found and were driven back to Airlie in a truck. Yo-Yo was treated for her injury and recovered.

ROCKY MOUNTAIN
POPULATION

PACIFIC COAST
POPULATION

INTERIOR
POPULATION

CURRENT REGIONAL POPULATIONS OF TRUMPETER SWANS

Cygnets usually make their first migration with their parents, so Yo-Yo, Isabelle and Sidney had made a good effort. Their success inspired another migration training flight a year later where, this time, sixteen trumpeter swans took part.

Today, there are about 20,000 trumpeter swans in the United States. Most of these birds nest in Alaska. Efforts are under way to bring the trumpeters back to marshes and lakes across America so some day the wild *ko-ho, ko-ho* call of the trumpeter may once again fill the skies.